401(k) Mastery

How to Set-Up, Grow, and protect your 401k

By Jim Hayne

Table of Contents

Preface

In 1981, a new television series called the Greatest American Hero hit the airwaves. The premise of the show centered on a regular guy working as a teacher (played by William Katt) receives an incredible gift from a group of aliens. This gift was a special red suit that allows the wearer to have special powers. Imagine having the ability to fly or have super strength, or to turn invisible, just by wearing a brightly colored red suit! The only problem was that our superhero immediately lost the instruction manual. The television series was mainly a comedy about our hero, learning how to activate the special powers this amazing suit.

In 1974, only seven years before the Greatest American Hero made its television debut, new legislation created a program to help the average individual, save for retirement. The 401K plan, allows individuals to put pre-tax money into a special investment account that defers any taxes due until distributions are made. Sounds great, unfortunately, like the television show Greatest American Hero, our legislators never encouraged any sort of instruction manual or classroom education in our high schools. The education is common sense to make available to help the average individual understand the investment options they have in their 401k plan. Just like in the television show, our leaders have given the American worker a potential benefit without the instruction manual. Whereas the television show was written as a comedy, it is no laughing matter that individuals are playing guessing games when it comes to their financial safety and the potential future strength of the United States as well.

That's what this educational manual is all about; to give you that education and knowledge to make better decisions with the choices you are given in your plan. Also, this manual will share how one wealth manager helped grow his client's retirement accounts.

One final note, this is not meant to be a comprehensive education, but one that should give most individuals a leg up on 90% of those that have never studied investing. Some of the information is based on fact, some based on my opinion, but all of the information shared here is to help you make better decisions with your retirement plan. If you are one that has little to no knowledge of investments or your 401(k) plan, then you should read the entire manual. If you feel you are fairly knowledgeable and are short of time, then move to the chapter 4 to learn how to discern which investments may be suitable for your situation, and which investments you will need to speed up, slow down, or park your portfolio.

If you find yourself making much better decisions regarding the returns and learning how to protect your returns in your retirement portfolio, then let me know. We all love to hear that effort in helping another person is appreciated! Let me know by sending an email to jimhayne@gmail.com.

Chapter 1   A little bit history!

Back in early 1930s when the depression was in full swing and unemployment was up around twenty-five percent, the United States government had introduced legislation called social security. Social Security was passed in 1935 and was designed to help calm the fears of many Americans and to protect them in their retirement. This legislation was presented as a safety net for the average working person when they reach the age of 65 and to help give confidence to all American's that the United States government would help provide support to them in their retirement.

In order to fund this program financially, the United States government required each working individual to pay a percentage of their paycheck that would be placed into a large pool of money set aside to pay for this program. The simple idea was the greater number of working Americans would be able to support the much smaller retirement force. From this pool of money, retirees would be provided an additional income meant to help support their retirement needs. This income was never meant to supply all needed income, but was meant to be a significant help to each individual. Looking back over 74 years, we realize Social Security isn't all that it was cracked up to be, and may not survive in its present form over the coming years.

In the 1950s, a worker may have been projected to receive $1200 a month in their Social Security payment. Because the average worker, according to the census reports in 1955, made under $3,500 in annual salary; $1200 a month was a lot of money. This larger than life number of $1200 a month artificially allowed people to believe they could live like Kings and Queens when they reached their retirement. Because there was very little education on how inflation impacted families, many Americans did not save any extra money for their retirement accounts. In the 1990s when many of these people actually did retire, $1200 a month was not enough to live comfortably. If these retirees did not have any other source of retirement savings, they would live more like a poor paupers then wealthy kings or queens.

 Many American's lack the understanding about the results of inflation on future spending; and unfortunately people today still make that same mistake. Inflation in its simplest form means that what a dollar can purchase today will get a lot less in the future! A simple example is found when you look at the cost of the United States postage stamp. In 1980 a United States postage stamp cost 15 cents, and in the year 2000, the United States postage stamp was 32 cents. In just 20 years the cost more than doubled, and it seems like we're looking to be on our way to double again since the cost of a stamp in 2019 is 55 cents.

Another income source for retirement many individuals relied upon was part of the benefit plan of a good company. If the company an individual worked for was large enough and had a pension plan in place, then the individual would have two sources of income, usually adequate to support their needs. Employees were told that if they worked hard for the company, kept doing what was told of them; and work for the company long enough they would be provided an income stream while they lived in their final years of retirement.

For a while this was wonderful, and it worked great at least in the beginning! However, as cost for healthcare increased, and people are living longer, companies that provided a pension, realized they could not keep pace paying people's retirement as they lived longer. The projections were completely unsustainable for the pension plans with their current investment holdings set aside. Since the drain on the pension program would only increase at an exponential rate, companies with the help of Congress made a change that removed their responsibility to fund future retirees and placed the responsibility on the individual worker. Thus, the 401(k) plan was born.

The longer life for our retirees is fundamental to understanding why Social Security is heading toward bankruptcy.

When Social Security started there were approximately 72 workers for every one retiree. Over the years as people lived longer, the percentage of workers vs. retirees shrank. Current studies show that we're down to six to eight workers for every one retiree, and the base of workers to retirees is still falling. Some studies tell us that there'll only be 2 to 3 workers for every retiree being paid in income from Social Security. The government tried to fix the problem by increasing the age from 65 to 67 to begin the benefit, but by the time our politicians got around to making this change, it was too late! Social Security, as we know it today, simply is an unsustainable system that neither political party; up to now has the backbone to face up to the needed steps to deal with problem. The politicians know that they will have to admit the truth. That truth being that another Government program that will not live up to its promises. Many people, though they have contributed to a plan to help themselves, have just given their money away to others and will probably never see much of their investment repaid to them. Social Security has become a process of using the income received today to support the expenses today, not setting aside enough money to keep the program financially healthy.

The politicians just keep avoiding solving the problem and wait for someone else to fix. Some people believe this is the worst scandal propagated against the average worker in the history of the United States. It seems to be like a government Ponzi scheme that went bad! Much worse than the scandals with Bernie Madoff that has lost people billions of dollars.

In the early 30s, People lived, on average, to the ripe old age of 62 years old. Some reports say 59 years of age; some reports say 62 years of age, regardless, people passed away before they would reach the age that Social Security would pay out a benefit at all. Politicians made a bet that most people would put in more money into the Social Security system, and never use it when they reached their retirement. So, for many years the politicians in both political parties used this money for other projects, thus not allowing this money is to grow as needed to support the growing retirement population.

As people started living longer and requiring more years in retirement, the pool of money that was set aside was not enough to continue the program indefinitely. Congress could no longer rely on this money to support the retiring public as promised. For too many years now, political promises have been made during every election year, but very little action has been taken. The lack of funds has been admitted in the Social Security update, located on the front page of the letter you receive from the Social Security department that arrives approximately 6 weeks before your birthday. In this letter, the IRS shares that they expect the pool of money to run out between the years of 1936 and 1940. Many people expect the program to be in trouble much sooner!

That is why this manual exists to help the average individual prepare themselves for their future retirement needs. My hope is that when you're done with an easy-to-read manual, you will gain knowledge that most Americans currently do not have. My desire is to teach you greater understanding of the variances between the investments and how to recognize the correct investment for your future retirement needs.

Chapter 2   401(k) Basics

In 1974, Congress passed new legislation called ERISA. This legislation created the 401(k) as we know it today. This legislation sounded good to the average citizen, it gave the individual worker the opportunity to invest in the stock market, with tax deferred growth to provide for their future retirement needs beyond what was going on in Social Security in or pensions.

This was the beginning steps of ending company responsibility in the form of pensions as we know it! The responsibility of providing a future retirement income was moving away from the corporations of the United States to the individual working person. In this one legislation, the United States Congress helped protect corporations from a future tsunami but they only increased the burden on the Social Security program. The politicians helped to get this legislation passed, by making everyone believe this was in their best interest. This could work if the individual worker had an education in investing. When we look back throughout history, Ibbotson's charted the average return in the stock market could be anywhere between two and twelve percent depending on the investment vehicle use. Since the government does not invest the money saved for Social security, the money has no chance to keep up with inflation!

My frustration with the legislative change is the politicians never provided an avenue for the average person to learn about how to invest in their 401(k). Yet we have had a program called a 401(k) for over 45 years. Yes, we have a traditional IRA or a simplified employment plan for those individuals that own their own businesses and a few other types of qualified plans available, but there has still been no education in middle school or high school to help prepare an to invest for their future. It's been 45 years since ERISA was created, and yet I believe over 75% of individuals are lacking knowledge on how much money they will need in their retirement account to support the lifestyle throughout their retired life. This thought is supported by a 2009 Retirement Confidence Survey created by the Employee Benefit Research Institute and Mathew Greenwald & Associates, Inc. in which they state 22% of the workers surveyed say they are not at all confident of their retirement, another 22% say they are not too confident, and 41% say they are somewhat confident. In all, 85% of the Retirement Confidence Survey state they are not very confident if they have enough money to retire comfortably. What is really interesting is the survey points out that 31% of those that felt very confident or somewhat confident have not saved any money for their retirement. That means the number of people who are confident will be surprised to find they are not going to live in retirement in comfort, so reality is confidence is misplaced.

In the many seminars, I have held over my 17 years of wealth management, to educate people in dealing with the stock market investing. I've often asked the simple question. How many of you were educated in the school system to help you invest. Rarely has a hand been raised, those that do raise their hand, will put them down when I will ask whether the investing class that taught you how to write a check or was the class that actually got into the nitty-gritty of the stock market and investing. There have only been a very few individuals who have had the benefit of a high school class that does discuss investing.

So, let us go over some basic questions:

Question #1 – Why call it a 401(k) plan?

The 401(k) refers to the location in the US tax code that shares the rules regarding the retirement plan. A 401 (k) is a plan only a company can offer to its employees. Thus, it is not available to an individual person unless they work for a company that offers such a plan. The rules in the IRS code refer to how to set up a retirement plan, how contributions are to be made, how much the contributions can be, how much the employer is allowed to match, how the tax treatment will be treated in regard to the contributions, and how and when distributions are to be made and the tax treatment the distributions will be treated. There are some specific rules on specific situations that are also in the code.

Question #2 – Why was the 401(k) plan created?

There are different beliefs about why the 401(k) plan was created. The most widely held belief is that individuals needed an additional source of income in retirement to make sure our retirees did not need to go on welfare. The favorable tax treatment of placing money into the plan, and the favorable tax deferred growth potential, was designed to be an incentive to employees to participate.   However, this author believes that the pension plans of the past were identified as unsustainable due to population growth.

With a larger and longer living population the future had more retirees living then workers to support, this would be devastating to the companies that offered pension plans. This is the same problem that social security is facing today! The IRS has mentioned the Social Security problem of running out of money somewhere in the late 2030's on the cover of the annual Social Security letter you receive a few months before your birthday. Have you read your social security letter lately? Anyhow, the reason the 401(k) was established was to move the responsibility of paying for the retirement of most Americans off many of the company's balance sheets, and move the responsibility to the individual American worker.

Question #3 – What is a 401(k) plan?

At the onset, the plan looks like it is a simple plan to understand, you put pretax money in, you choose investments found inside the plan, and the money grows without taxes being assessed to the growth, and when you take out the distributions in retirement, you will finally be taxed. However, over the years the plans have grown to be more complex in choices and with different fee structures. More rules have been established to control when you can take money out, and even how often you can make changes to your investments.

The key advantage of a retirement plan is the pretax contributions and the ability to have the account grow tax-deferred allowing for compounding of growth upon growth. This simple ability should allow a plan to grow much faster and allow the retiree possible hundred thousand if not millions dollars more over time.

Question #4 – How do I put money into a 401(k) plan?

If a company has a 401(k) plan, you can begin investing into the plan by simply having a percentage or dollar amount directed from your paycheck. However, some companies have a waiting period before you can enroll. Often the enrollment is set for two times a year; Once on January 1st and on July 1st. Another qualification may be centered on the hours worked per week, excluding part time employees from the plan. The reason, it cost the employer money for every employee participating.

Question #5 – How do I get money out of my 401(k) plan?

This could be complicated. Every 401(k) plan has a plan document that outlines the distribution rules. Some plans allow loans, some don't. Most plans are tough to get money out until you reach the magical age of 59 ½ where you can get the money out without a penalty. The penalty the government places on your money is 10% if you do not meet tough requirements. This 10% penalty is in place to help insure that individuals use this plan for retirement as intended and not a savings account vehicle for other things. Because the government knows it will not have enough money to take care of the growing number of retiring individuals, because they are living longer; the government is allowing for less tax dollars to be deferred and therefore lost to the current tax bucket. That is why penalties are in place and why you should try to keep every dollar in the plan until retirement.

Chapter 3   Bottom line how is a 401(k) plan going to help me?

Imagine tomorrow is the day you retire. You are ready for the last part of your life to be relaxing and full of the dreams you have had spending time doing what you want, without a job dictating your schedule. However, you soon find out that everything you want to do is more expensive then you had planned on so many years ago. You may not be able to do all the vacations and activities you want, in the glory years, for fear of outliving your money.

Having a retirement investment account like a 401(k) is one of the best ways to set aside a lump sum of money in order to provide a monthly income when your income from a job stops. Yet, just putting the money into your retirement plan, is not a plan. Putting money aside is one important step toward having a chance at having more than enough money in retirement. However, the most important step is having the knowledge to make good choices so your investments make more than the money market fund and beat inflation.

I have heard from many people that they are afraid of losing any money so they take the safe approach and invest in the money market, or only bond funds. This is fine if you do not need much money from this retirement plan for living income during retirement. However, most people do not have any other source of income other than Social Security, and that may not be available as expected in the future.

So, it begs the question, what will you do if you do not have enough money when you are ready to retire, or worst have to retire before you are willing due to bad health or bad job market and being laid off. Some people choose to work full or part time for a few more years longer than planned; or until you die; having your income continue to be provided by a paycheck like you have all your life. You could learn to live on less than planned and have the money stretch out longer. You could invest to try to get a higher return on your money, but most people realize the higher the return sought, the more risk one is taking on. Finally, you can depend on your children to take care of any shortfall and move in with your kid's family.

If these choices are not satisfactory, then you need to plan on having enough money to supply the monthly need. So do you know how much money you will need at your desired retirement age to keep you comfortable through retirement? Since you do not have a crystal ball, and therefore do not know the day you will die, or the actual market return you will average in the future, you will need to make some assumptions. One assumption is the age at retirement, another is the annual average rate of return, still another is knowing if you will live out retirement healthy or unhealthy therefore needing more money for medical expenses, finally you will need to guess at when you will die. The only real assumption you can possibly improve, with education, is your average rate of return by learning how to improve your investment return in your plan.

Have you ever heard of the rule of 72? Simply put, it is a way to determine how many years it should take to double your money. If I invested ten thousand dollars on January 1st 2010, how many years will it take to have it be worth twenty thousand dollars with a nine percent average return?

If, I divide seventy-two by nine I would get 8 years.   9 / 72 = 8

 If your portfolio averaged twelve percent it would take six years. 12 / 72 = 6

If you only get money market returns and I am being nice by saying it is three percent (currently it is less than one percent at the time of this writing) it would take twenty-four years to double. 4 / 72 = 24

Consistent good performance is necessary to provide the growth you will need to have for your portfolio to grow substantially to outpace both taxes and inflation.

By investing regularly into a your 401(k) plan you can have taxed deferred growth compounded annually that will help you provide an monthly stream of income to provide the type of retirement you may dream about. But let me give you some numbers of how a tax deferred plan works vs. a taxable plan.

Let's assume you are 35 years old, able to put five hundred dollars into your plan every year for thirty years. Assuming you are in the twenty five percent tax bracket, here are the results. One point I would like to make here is that the calculators assume an annual return of the same amount every year. This does not happen in real life so this is only an example of possible returns. Your portfolio will be more or less based on the investment return!

Assuming a 6% annual return; 30 years; $500 monthly or $6,000 annual amount.

Tax-deferred result   = $ 502,810

Taxable result   = $ 382,514

That's a $120,296 or a 24% difference. However, if you tax the amount at 25% you would still have $ 422,108 or almost an extra 40k.

Assuming a 7% annual return; 30 years; $500 monthly or $6,000 annual amount.

Tax-deferred result   = $ 606,438

Taxable result   = $ 438,027

That's a $168,411 or a 28% difference. However, if you tax the amount at 25% you would still have $ 499,829 or almost an extra 61k.

Assuming a 8% annual return; 30 years; $500 monthly or $6,000 annual amount.

Tax-deferred result   = $ 734,075

Taxable result   = $ 502,810

That's a $231,265 or a 31.5% difference. However, if you tax the amount at 25% you would still have $ 595,556 or almost an extra 93k.

Assuming a 9% annual return; 30 years; $500 monthly or $6,000 annual amount.

Tax-deferred result   = $ 891,451

Taxable result   = $ 578,478

That's a $312,973 or a 35 % difference. However, if you tax the amount at 25% you would still have $ 713,588 or a little more than extra 135k extra.

As you can see for every single percent gain per year, your returns are greatly enhanced. This is why this education is so important to your future retirement. It is simply one of the most important reasons to have every American understand how to manage their retirement plan. With understanding and knowledge we can expect greater results, yet, it is very frustrating that this is not taught in our schools. If our nation is filled with financially sound individuals, our nation will be financially stronger.

If you want to have great results in your 401(k) as determined by your returns, then you need to focus on learning about the investment sub accounts found in your personal retirement plan. What I will not focus on is issues with your Human Resource person, or the issue with weather your plan allows loans or not, or if the boss is planning on matching any contributions you put in.

I want to focus on the one element that this book can help make a difference in your financial life, the most important and often the one factor for your retirement success, ending up with much more money than you would have if you did not read this book.

My goal is to make the investment in this book a pittance compared to the huge difference your retirement balance will become.

Why is it when you sit in your companies 401(k) plan meeting held at least annually, that the person discussing your plan tells you why it is important to contribute to your retirement (and it is important); why it is important to know about inflation and how things will cost more in the future (and it is important); why waiting is bad for your ending dollar amount (and they are right!); but they don't spend any decent time discussing the choices you have other than to connect them on a risk scale and tell you to choose the right allocation based on your age and time you have before retiring. Many of the presentations color code the investment choices based on the risk and volatility of the investment, then give you a percentage of your total portfolio to put into that risk level. With many investments that are the same risk classification, how do you know which investment is the better investment. Many times most of the investments flat out stink. Most retirement plans have both good and bad investments to choose from, this book is all about learning how to determine the better investment for your portfolio.

Because I have been that guy that had given the talk for many years, I know that most of the people standing in front of you are not able to discuss specifics investment choices for fear of miscommunication and risk of retaliation of a lawsuit. Many of the agents giving presentations are not even licensed with a series 7, they only have a series 6 which is often obtained by insurance agents to be able to sell these investments, so they give practical advice on the reason and need to be involved, give advice on sign up procedure, but no advice is often given on making the most of your investment returns. That is why this book has been written. If I do a good job helping you understand the basics, you will be able to see the fund selections for what they really are; The Good, The Bad, and the Ugly!

If there is one desire that I wish I could accomplish is that I would help everyone understand that simply having money in a mutual fund investment is all anyone has to do to have it make money is worthless advice. Truth is-there is very few lucky successful investors, more often it is educated successful investors that do well in their investing. So which investor do you want to be? My guess is that you want to be the lucky successful investor who does very little but has great rewards- good luck on that! The best chance of adding hundreds of extra dollars to your monthly income, is learning more about your investment choices.

Did you just read the above sentence and say to yourself, a few extra hundred dollars will not make a big difference? If you reread the above the sentence you will notice I said adding hundreds of extra dollars to your monthly income, in order to have monthly income grow by hundreds, you need tens to hundreds of thousands extra in your portfolio generating the monthly income. That is what I am talking about, getting over the fear of making mistakes, and to put have your money work as hard as you do, so you can have a chance to enjoy your final years without fear of running out of money.

If I could do one thing to help strengthen this country it would be to help educate everyone with basic investment knowledge contained here, to help each person be wealthier and wiser when it comes to investments. I also realize this book is written for the beginning and intermediate investor. The advanced investor may learn a few ideas, but the educated person probably will make more return just because they have taken time to have a greater understanding of investments.

If each person in America had more dollars in their retirement account and even in their savings accounts, the whole nation would be stronger! Do you doubt this? Think about how so many defaults and misplaced risk has damaged our economy for years, in fact many investment indexes have a ten year negative number as of 2010. Simply put, if you invested in the index like the S + P 500 prior to 2010, your investment would not have any percentage gain, you will have many more shares of the index allowing for a stronger growth spurt when the index finally does rise, but the ten years prior to 2010 has been a decade of slow returns. If you understand investing, the main people hurt are those that need to start taking retirement income during the slow time, not allowing the large share holding to grow in the future. Since 2010 the average return has been around 10% allowing for the ups and downs of the market.

You have heard it before, but more time in the market allowing for the ups and downs, should allow for a better return performance, then if you have a shorter investment horizon. Why? It is just that you have more money growing tax deferred and the growth has time to compound and grow at a exponential rate. Look at the numbers below to see some simple examples to help prove this concept.

Year 1- deposit of $5,000 beginning of the year and having a 8% growth = $ 5,400

Year 2- deposit an additional $5,000 beginning of the year and having a 8% growth = $ 11,232

Year 3- deposit an additional $5,000 beginning of the year and having a 8% growth = $ 17,530.56

Year 4- deposit an additional $5,000 beginning of the year and having a 8% growth = $ 24,333.05

Year 5- deposit an additional $5,000 beginning of the year and having a 8% growth = $ 31,679.65

Year 6- deposit an additional $5,000 beginning of the year and having a 8% growth = $ 39,614.02

Year 7- deposit an additional $5,000 beginning of the year and having a 8% growth = $ 48,183.14

Year 8- deposit an additional $5,000 beginning of the year and having a 8% growth = $ 57,437.79

Year 9- deposit an additional $5,000 beginning of the year and having a 8% growth = $ 67,432.81

Year 10- deposit an additional $5,000 beginning of the year and having a 8% growth = $ 78,227.44

Deposits = $50,000   Growth on earnings = $28,227.44

Now over the next ten years stronger dollar growth happens. And the results are:

Year 20- deposit an additional $5000 beginning of each year with annual 8% growth = $ 247,112.61

Deposits = $100,000   Growth on earnings = $147,112.61

The following year the growth in dollars based on the same 8% and a $5000 deposit at the beginning of the year is $ 25,171.17 in that year alone. The growth in dollars of year eleven with same $5000 deposit and 8% growth would have only been $ 11,658.20. Imagine what the following five years would be after year twenty but instead of 8% you received a 11% because you have been managing your portfolio, and because you have been managing this portfolio, your results happened to average 3% average per year. The results would be huge. My point is simple. The markets never give the same percent each and every year, it is volatile, and performance will vary because of volatility, but your involvement with some understanding of better choices, will defiantly make a huge difference in your profits, and therefore your retirement.

What is a mutual fund? It is simply a grouping of individual investments chosen by a representative hired by a fund family to buy and sell investments in a large way to help lower trading cost verses you individually purchasing your individual investments. Often, a mutual fund allows for a greater purchase of different investments at one purchase price, and with a representative hired by the fund family to trade the fund for your, you would expect a more experienced result. However, this is not always the result of a mutual fund. Because there are more mutual funds then individual investment choices, the mutual fund world is full of individual that do not have the experience or the ability to do a good job. Many with experience find it difficult, and have periods of bad returns. But with so many bad funds, there are incredible funds too. That is why funds are so popular with the masses, professional management, with little cost up front, and really not much time involved in putting your money to work, since you are hiring another group to do this for you.

So what are the some of the features one should look at to decide if a fund is good or bad? Realizing all investments are not the same, everyone has to ask certain questions to help filter out the worse choices. However, even after the filters are used, some investments that look good may not perform exactly the same moving forward. Since we do not have a crystal ball, we do not know what he future holds. Realizing that past performance does not equal future return is important, but looking at past performance is really one of our best measures to decide on a good investment. It is similar to picking good players for your fantasy sports team, you go by past performance, and occasionally the players do not perform as well as they have in the past due to a new team dynamic and other outside factors.

One of the best filters used to determine the right investment choice is observing the long term performance against the proper index associated with the investment. You want to make sure you are using the correct index or the measure is useless. Measuring the performance of a small capitulation fund against a fixed income index would make the fund look dramatically different. It would be like comparing the top speed of a tricycle to a racing car. But some may argue the racing car may crash, and therefore the tricycle is a better performer. To this I say the better the driver, the better the driver can handle the top speeds that can occur on the track. This is a basic but important principal that outlines the concept I have been trying to get people to understand. Yes, the fixed income fund may not crash, but it moves so slow that it will never help a person win the prize, or in this case win enough dollars in your plan to make retirement a reality according to your goals, dreams and desires.

Another great way to determine a good fund is the history of a Manager or Team of managers and length of tenure in both markets and with the fund represented. Having a manager that has a great track record for one fund does not always mean a new endeavor will be successful. However, it is an easy signal you have a good investment when the manager or manager team and the fund have been together for over ten years and the performance is good as well. Most investments like mutual funds or managed money funds, will not make it big news when they change their investment managers. Why? Well how would you feel if you were used to a financial advisor you have worked with for over twenty years just retired and your firm you have been with sends you a letter saying your new advisor is a new person you have never met. Are you excited? Probably not, and that is why the companies you invest with do not make it a big news flash. So, my point is having a good manager or team is great, but you need to check on them regularly to make sure they are still there.

Fund objectives is another feature most people do not read but should. Understanding what the fund is trying to achieve I think is important to know if you are going to put your hard earned money into it. More importantly the investment objectives will help you know if the investments chosen are more aggressive or more conservative in relation to the other choices in the same category. Simply put, if a choice is in the growth and income category but the investments chosen are more apt to give growth rather than income, you can argue that the investment is more aggressive than a similar fund that is focused on more income than on growth. Knowing the risk associated inside the category can help you understand why one investment may be getting higher returns in some years and much lower returns in another verse an investment that focus on income with a more consistent record. It is important to use this qualifier to see if the investment managers are taking on little or much risk in achieving those objectives even inside the category.

Fees and costs associated with the investment are often the ongoing expenses that are not easily determined by posted expected cost can bring down performance. I don't have any problem paying a little extra for good service, in fact many times quality is only found when you are willing to buy from quality advice, and great does not often come cheap. But many funds are so similar that the performance is going to be similar, and if one fund has higher ongoing expenses, then your performance will be less than the other. Often you will find an investment that is meant to mirror the S + P 500 index. It never actually does as well as the index, because of the fees to pay the manager and trading costs. The index is only a index without any cost so it is hard to beat in these funds. Yet I have seen some management funds charge as much as two percent or more to buy and sell investment trying to mirror the investment. So if the investment index averages ten percent a year, this fund will return only eight percent. Over time two percent per year will be devastating to your overall return as mentioned earlier so do keep an eye on expenses so you can get what you deserve, and pay only what is fair.

If you are attempting to find an more aggressive investment to outperform an index, you need to focus less on consistency and more on the performance during volatile times. Simply put how does the investment perform when the market is in a strong move upward, together with how is the investment performing when the market is in a strong move down. Upside momentum and

Downside momentum during volatile times can make or break returns for an investment. If the market index like the S + P 500 moves up twenty percent in a short time, and your investment goes up over twenty percent like twenty-five percent that would be great, but more than often when the market goes down in a short time, the same investment may outpace the index on this side as well. Often, if the index is at twenty percent down in the short period, the investment falls even faster than the upside, like thirty or more percent. That is why I like to find funds that may not perform as well as the index on the upside in a short move only because it really protects better on the downside. So in number terms, if the market rises twenty percent in a short period, then my investment must get at least seventy-five percent of the return, or in this case fifteen percent or more only if the same investment protects the downside better than the upside or only loses fifty percent to seventy-five percent of the downside or less. So getting most of the upside and losing less than half of the downside is ideal. Why does this work, there are more dramatic down turns then upside movements, we know over time the market seems to move up, but I am focusing on those dramatic moves. Because this strategy makes its money on the down turns, or better said, loses less money then the overall market. It turns out that it makes more return over time. Because it is hard to actually see the benefits during downturns because we naturally only see the losses and do not really compare at this time, it is not very popular to say "hey isn't it great we only lost ten percent because the market lost more, most people only hear we lost ten percent! Since the market is like a heartbeat and does go up and down on a regular basis, I can really do well to lose less and there for not have as far to go up to get to even. This works great as long as the market recovers, which it always has, but sometimes people do not believe the recovery is possible, and so people panic. This is why the wealthy seem to make more than those that do not have as much to invest, simply because they do not have emotions attached to the process.

Let's make up numbers to support this thought.

Market movement	Index	Difference
+20%	+16%	- 4%
-20%	-13%	+ 7%
+12%	+ 9%	- 3%
-12%	- 6%	+ 6%
+10%	+ 8%	- 2%
-10%	- 6%	+ 4%
		+ 8%

Learn to ask good questions like:

How long has the fund been around?

What index should you compare your investment against?

How long has the manager been a manager and how long with the particular investment?

How much is the fund charging in upfront and ongoing fees?

How does the investment return on up years compare to the corresponding index?

How does the investment return on down years compare to the corresponding index?

Chapter 4   Driving your 401k

Learning about investing in your 401(k) plan is like learning to drive a car. First you must learn about the different gears and when you should put the correct gear into place while driving during different speeds and conditions. A car also has brake pedal and a gas pedal which needs to be used properly or you will be hurt. Driving a car safely requires proper use of a parking brake, foot brake, gears one through five and of course the neutral setting.

Most retirement plans have pre-selected mutual funds to choose from, some others have company stock as a choice, and few have the ability for the employee to buy any stock sold on a particular exchange. No matter what choices your plan offers, you need to learn to drive your 401(k) plan properly which will require you to learn how each investment is expected to perform during different conditions.

One key to driving your 401(k) is determining what blend of investments match the different gears of driving a manual transmission car. Putting it another way is simply know if the investment is a first gear investment only meant to give low consistent return or a more aggressive investment meant to represent the fifth gear running fast and with greater overall performance potential. However, with greater performance means the potential for greater risk of crashing at faster speeds, allowing for more potential harm to the portfolio. When you drive your car from home to work, you must use different gears during the trip, working the gears to produce the desired speed weather you are leaving your driveway, or driving on freeway. However, driving a portfolio is not just having one investment speed, but mixing up the different gears at the same time to get a smoother drive. The combination of the proper investments is designed to help your retirement ride be much smoother with greater results.

Let's connect the types of investments to the different gears of a car.

Park - Cash, Money Market, Money Market Investments

(Investments similar to the bank where you can get your money quickly if needed.)

1st Gear- 100% Income, Corporate Bond Investments, Government Bond Investments

(Income producing investments that allow for income rather than growth of principal)

2nd Gear- Balanced Position (Has Some Bonds and Some Equity)

(Mixing Income producing Investments with some dividend paying stocks attempting to grow the portfolio with income and growth.)

3rd Gear- Dividend paying equity, Growth and Income Investments

(Using larger company stocks that have a dividend paid to the stock holder as an incentive to purchase a stock that has been around and more established but expected to grow slower than younger and smaller companies.)

4th Gear- Growth Stocks, Large Cap and Mid Cap Growth
Investments

*(Stocks where the companies are still expected to grow and
therefore do not give much if any dividends. These stocks tend to
be more volatile than the stocks giving dividends.)*

5th Gear- Small Cap Growth Stocks, Aggressive Growth
Investments or Emerging Growth Investments

*(Stocks where the companies are younger and smaller so they tend
to have greater upside potential, but also is expected to have more
volatility then other stocks that are larger and have been more
established.)*

This is very simplistic model, we will need to go deeper into
understanding the different investments, and how their objectives
and goals will help or hurt your portfolio.

First, all investors need to understand where they are going or how
long it will take to get there. It is a map to their retirement
destination. You have probably heard the story of the person who
did not map out their trip and arrived in the wrong place. Not only
do you need a road map on your destination, but you need to know
how long you have to get there. If your time is short you may need
to travel by plane, rather than a car, or if you have the time, maybe
a nice yacht would be your choice. Obviously, we need to know if
we are close to arrival because if you are within five years of your
retirement age, or just starting out on a long journey and you have

thirty years to go before you desire to slow down. Whatever the case is for you, the way you drive your retirement is one important key. Why?

I remember one investor asking me to fix his retirement account after a massive painful drop in the market. I, as always wanted to create a complete financial health assessment to understand the details beyond performance of his portfolio. When I completed the assessment I realized this investor had not only been on track to retire he had enough to retire two years earlier, he could have done so with extra to spare. However, in the last twenty months he had lost a large percentage of his portfolio, he had the amount of money needed to retire and now it was not there. He needed about 1.2 million dollars and he had over 1.5 million prior to the down turn.

The problem he had was that he did not slow down the portfolio as he neared retirement; in fact he kept allowing his advisor to drive his portfolio in fifth gear and basically went off a cliff. When he showed me his most recent statement he had $372,000 left. In just two years from having over 1.5 million he lost about 70% of his retirement portfolio. Ouch!

When putting together an appropriate portfolio with realistic expectations I knew he would not like the plan placed before him and he would not want to take my advice. Why? The portfolio would take over nine years to get back to where it needed to be in order to retire. He did thank me for my time and walked away. I suspected he wanted an advisor to repair the portfolio back to its original size in the same time frame it was lost in. I have often wondered if he found an advisor that told him what he wanted to hear, and because the following year was even worse than the two prior, if he lost another chunk of his portfolio. I will never know, but I do hope the best for him!

When you drive a car off the cliff, you can't aim the car back up at the cliff and expect it to fly back to the location of the accident. We have to understand and respect certain laws like gravity and gravity does work with investments as well.

The trick to arriving safe to your destinations is to minimize the risk along the way! When we get into a car we are taking a risk no matter how safe the car design is and how cautious we are in driving the car. Driving your portfolio to fast or to slow is potential danger for you and those around you. The bottom line is that you need to drive properly and within stated boundaries.

For any trip over terrain that we are unfamiliar with, it is wise to obtain a map to better understand the roads to take as well as any possible obstacles to a direct route. Looking to see if there are shortcuts that are available, and glimpsing into the possible places to avoid and or rest when needed. I remember taking a trip north from Southern California to Central California. According to the map, I could save time by driving up the 5 freeway (you can tell I grew up in California, since we put "the" in front of the freeway number) and then cutting across to get on the 101 to my destination. However, there were a few choices on when to make the move over to the 101 freeway. The one that was the closest to my destination was the one I choose because it was seemed the shortest and quickest. When I took the trip and turned onto the transition, it was so curvy and set around so many hills and mountains that it actually took longer than if I had taken another transition that was further from my destination but would have saved a good thirty minutes.

When you plan your trip, you could break down the travel time in regard to the percentage of driving time you would use in different gears. For a long distance trip, obviously you would use higher gears most of the time, and for a shorter trip, the lower gears would be used more often. If you map the percentage of time using the different gears, you may see an example like, 5% using the brakes, 10% using the first gear, 10% using the second gear, 30% using the third gear, 30% using the fourth gear, and 15% using the fifth gear. This is true of the retirement plan investments too. If you have more time, and your ability to handle high speeds is acceptable, then you may be using equity in a much higher percentage. Maybe your trip is exactly the same as the example above and so your portfolio would look like this : 5% Cash, 10% Income, 10% Balanced, 30% Growth and Income, 30% Growth, and 15% in Emerging Growth or Aggressive Growth. Obviously the trip whether in a car, or for your retirement, is dependent on your ability to handle higher speeds and understanding how much time on the road you will need to travel toward your goal.

Let's take a closer look at the investments in each category, understand the investment a little more in detail, and help investors know how much gas to put on the pedal for their personal situation.

When you get into a car the car should be stopped and placed in park. Usually the parking brake would be in place to keep the car from moving. At times when driving on the freeway you will apply the brakes when traffic slows down, and if you live in the Los Angeles area, you will need to stop repeatedly along the way if you leave at a time when people are driving to or from work. Applying the brake or placing the car in park is for one simple reason, you need to keep from moving or you will hit something or someone unintended. So let's look at how the cash and money market investments perform this function.

Putting on the Brake or Parking:

Cash and or Money Market Investments are the lowest risk investments available. The primary objective is to protect the capital placed into the investment and to give some, often very little, income too. The investment will accomplish this by investing in money market securities, and very short term loans made to banks. The NAV (Net asset value) is the price you can buy and sell each share or unit for this being set at $ 1.00 per share. An investment in a money market fund is not insured or guaranteed by the Federal Deposit Insurance Corporation or any government agency. Although the Fund seeks to preserve the value of your investment at $1.00 per share, it is possible to lose money investing in the Fund.

With money market mutual funds the purchase price should be $1.00 per share, and is designed to stay at the one dollar per share price. The growth for this mutual fund is the income percentage the fund is currently paying. Currently, as of this writing in 2010; money market are paying the lowest rates I have witnessed in the market. The main reason for the money market is to not lose money in a down market, or to park some money to use later when the market does go down, and you want to take advantage of a better time to purchase more aggressive positions.

One easy way to identify which of the mutual fund in your 401(k) choices is the money market fund is to look for the five letter symbol that is used as a fund symbol. In reality each investment has a number called a cusip number that is the true marker like a social security number for each individual. The cusip is a long address that often uses both numbers and letters. To make an easier moniker, Wall Street created the five letter address.   The money market fund will end with two XX's. So the money market symbol will look like * * * XX with the * representing alphabetic letters connected to a mutual fund. A mutual fund has different ways of being represented in the newspaper, some use the five symbols, and others use a reference to the name.

Money market funds are used to keep money safer than other investments. However, some managers running the fund may take on extra risk by leaning toward the more aggressive short term forms of money management instruments. There have been a few times in our history that money market funds almost went below the $1.00 NAV because of this practice, but government leadership realizing the loss of confidence that would be fostered, stepped in and helped to make sure the money market stayed at the $1.00.

 Because Money market funds are pretty safe, but there is always a chance a fund my lose value and cause the one dollar NAV to be in jeopardy. The mutual fund prospectus does have a warning: The warnings are all very similar and states similar warnings.

"Investors should carefully consider a fund's investment goals, risks, charges, and expenses before investing. To obtain a prospectus, which contains this and other information about a fund, please contact your investment representative or call the investment company directly. Please read the prospectus carefully before investing or sending money."

 I will put the common warnings in my words and paraphrase: No assurance it will work, not insured, not guaranteed by anyone. Though it is considered safer than other investments, it may not work and you may lose money.

How's that for covering themselves! However, most professionals agree that the United States Government would have to have a collapse of the financial system to have a money market investment suffer. However, this has almost happened in recent history!

So, if you are investing into the money market investment you want only to get a very low return but do not wish to lose any principal. This is mainly for protecting your portfolio during a downturn.

Money market investments are not a place to invest for any prolonged period and should be avoided since the return is so low.

1st Gear- 100% Income Investments

The first gear with a car is simply designed to give you greater ability to move your car forward without taking on too much speed. Income investments can also be used when you move closer to retirement to lower the risk, and give a more comfortable ride. You would never drive your car only in 1st gear, but this is a very important gear for you to master in order to have any effective driving experience.   This is the one gear that puts forth forward motion and meant for a small distance of travel. Without the 1st gear, your car would not move very smooth, and jumping into second gear immediately is often very choppy and not very healthy for an engine to do continuously.

Income Investments are simply meant to create income and this is very necessary for investors that have a need to take a monthly paycheck. Income Investments are the second lowest risk of investing. The primary objective is to provide a high level of income and a lower risk of principal loss then compared to an equity investment. The investment will accomplish this by investing in a diversified portfolio of bond securities.

With Income funds the NAV will change daily to represent the underlying bond securities in the portfolio. The change of NAV for this mutual fund is based on what the underlying bonds could be sold for day by day. Individual bonds will fluctuate in price due to the current interest rates, bond quality ratings, and the percentage of interest they will pay.

Not all Income funds are the same! While one Incomes fund purchases government bonds, another may purchase global or international bonds. Some portfolio managers will purchase high quality corporate bonds; some with short durations others with long durations. Still other portfolio managers will purchase high yielding bonds or mortgage securities. Still others purchase municipals or tax free bonds. As you can see from this list, each Income fund has different income potential and different risk associated with the principal invested.

Having an Income fund purchase US Treasury Bonds will often be considered safe compared to a high yield bond fund. The fund with lower risk often has the lower the rate of income. Because income is what is desired, many believe that you should buy different types of Income funds to properly diversify.

Some Income funds have different bonds with a range from short to long maturity dates, in an attempt to get higher yield without giving up to much on risk. Other investment managers may use a mix of styles like government and corporate to get greater results. These investments will show the allocation of bonds in each ratings class. There are two main rating agencies that put out letter grades to help investors understand the level of risk associated with a company. S & P uses letters with all uppercase like AAA or

BBB. Moody's is another agency that uses a combination of upper
and lower case letters to demonstrate its grading system.
"AAA/Aaa" (S & P/Moody's) rating is the highest where the "A/a"
rating is lower than AAA/Aaa but still considered high quality.
Ratings follow a grading scale where "A" rating is high and "C" is
considered junk. Junk bonds are bonds that have a higher risk
rating and a stronger possibility that the company the bond
represents will go out of business and leave the investor with the
possibility of losing their principal. As an example the rating chart
may look like this:

S & P / Moody's	
Rating	% Of Total Net Assets
AAA/Aaa	43.3 %
AA/Aa	28.5 %
A/A	12.4 %
BBB/Baa	7.5 %
BB/Ba	5.2%
B/B	3.1 %

Investment wisdom says you should have bonds in your portfolio to help diversify your holdings and risk. Often, when the equity market begins to suffer, the Income portfolios will gain in value. This happens because more investors are fleeing from the equity positions and purchasing the bond instruments. With supply and demand still a real driver to returns, the investments in bonds will go up because people are buying and sellers realize they can get higher prices for their positions they are selling. The opposite is true too! When the equity markets are doing well, often the bond values will drop in value because there are now more sellers and the demand is moving away from these investments.

The idea here is to have bonds act like a shock absorber for your portfolio. Any comfortable riding car will have good shock absorbers to cushion the occupants from bumps in the road. A good portfolio will need to determine how comfortable they are willing to be on their financial ride.

Some believe you should have a percentage of Incomes equal to half your age. These investors believe that if you were fifty years old, you should have 25% allocation to bonds in your portfolio. While this may be a benefit to some, I believe the determining factor should focus more about how close to your retirement you are and it would be important to include all your potential income sources to understand more about your cash flow, tax implication and cash flow need that has to be met.

2nd Gear   Balanced Investments - Has Bonds And Equity

The second gear of a car is used to begin speeding up to transition your car to the higher gears. Likewise the balanced investments utilize a cautious and more balanced approach to investing. The primary objective is to produce a greater amount of income with a second objective of growth. A balanced investment uses both bonds and dividends from equity, convertible stocks and preferred stocks, which allows for some protection of capital but allows for a little more upside potential then a straight bond investment.

Balanced investments usually have an allocation of bonds to equity with many having a sixty percent income to forty percent equity to have a mixture of both income and larger dividend paying equity positions. Some investments have the higher percentage leaning toward the equity, some to the bonds. Either way the balanced investment is meant to give the investor a smoother performance with less volatility then a straight equity investment.

In 401(k) plans the balanced investment could be the one stop shop for investors that do not want to do much work on thinking about their investments. Some investors pick an asset allocation investment that puts a group of investments together in one investment, and labels the investment conservative, balanced or aggressive. So whether you choose a balanced investment or an asset allocation investment the primary focus is a position that is in transition from straight income and straight equity.

However, I often like to remind investors that it is still about performance overall and every 1 percentage greater annual return an investor receives over time can significantly impact you future dollars available.

For example: If you invested $500 every month for twenty years and averaged an 8% return, you will have $ 296,473 dollars in twenty years. However, if you had a return of 9% instead, you will have $ 336,448 dollars in twenty years. That is a difference of almost $ 40,000. Just for fun if you averaged a 10% return for the same twenty year period, you will have $ 382,848 or over $ 86,000 dollars more than at 8%. That is why taking a few minutes to understand, strategize, and implement these instructions could make or break your future.

Balanced investments can be a great place to invest a small portion if you are looking to be a little more aggressive than investing in straight bond investments. However, to maximize your account you should not invest only in these types of investments. The only place I would like to have an investor use a balance investment is in place of a growth and income investment.

3rd Gear- Growth and Income Investments

The third gear of a car is used to drive with more torque and ability to get better performance, meaning the third gear is used to drive up hills, or to drive at a level pace using lower speeds. Likewise the growth and income investment utilize larger capitalization stocks with the desire to have less volatile positions. More Consistent performance is what makes the investment a valuable election choice.

The growth and income investment is one that will give the benefits income and growth, but the income is derived more from dividends then income from bonds interest. Usually the focus leans to growth over income so some who are considered moderate may select this investment strategy. Meaning if a year performance was ten percent, then their income part of the equation may be 1.5% - 4% with the remainder of the performance being generated by the growth portion of the allocation.

The third gear Growth and Income Investment are in my opinion, the core to your success of investing within many portfolios. The primary objective is to grow the portfolio through investments that are typically large capitalization that pay a dividend. One rule I have come to realize is that if an investment has equity as its holding and pays more than 1.5 % in income, consider it a growth and income investment. In order to accomplish this, the investment can invest in convertible securities, preferred stocks as well as common stock positions.

When it comes to equity investments, large capitalization stock is considered to be the more conservative position when we are focusing on equity only. Large capitalization stocks usually have been around for awhile and are more likely a name you have heard before. The large capitalization stocks are more apt to pay a dividend, because they have grown the company to a point where its growth momentum has slowed. So to keep the shareholders happy, they pay a dividend which is annual income that often is taxed better then straight income from fixed income investments.

Getting a more consistent return compared to the stronger volatility of growth investments or aggressive growth investments is why growth and income investments are so important. Most people enjoy fast rides at amusement parks. But if you were to connect investment types to rides at Disneyland, I would connect Bond investments to the merry-go-round where you are not moving higher just at an easy pace where smiling and waving at the family every twenty seconds is the norm. Growth and Income investments would be more of a ride like Dumbo flying elephants, where you can get a little speed and has a button to move up in the air and get a little more air in the hair. Growth Investments are more like the Matterhorn bobsled ride or California Screamin where you move quickly over tracks and may even do a flip. Aggressive investments are like the Tower of Terror where you are sitting in a seat, but when the plunge happens you are held down only by the seatbelt, and then after falling the ride takes you right back up for another fall or two.

One potential problem with many employees when having to choose their investments from a list in their retirement plan is they pick the investment with the greatest return over the last five years without any other consideration. The issue is that the best performing strategies often rotate every few years or so, and when you pick a investment that has done well over the last few years, it often does not do as well over the next few years.

Many experts will talk about a growth over a value season, or value strategies over a growth strategies for a given time period, but just because growth is doing well now, does not mean the value positions, which is where growth and income investments preside, are not making money. In fact, history over the last twenty years shows the value investments over time seem to do a little bit better against their growth partners. Growth and Income investments are typically more of a consistent return that I believe most investors want.

4ᵗʰ Gear- Growth Investments

Many cars devote most of their time driven in higher gears and use the lower gears only when necessary. The main reason for moving to the higher gears is that you get on a freeway because you have a long distance to travel and need higher performance during this portion of the trip. However, many drivers use the forth gear for a shorter period and never need the higher gear. This can be true of Growth Investments as well. Growth investments are higher risk and will also have a higher volatility within a portfolio. The primary objective is to grow capital placed into the investment with little or no desire for income.

Growth investments desire to have strong performance by investing in growth securities that are expected to grow faster than other investments securities in the same category. Many times the growth will be focused on companies that are more mid to large capitalization in regard to the company financial size and we find specially those that have been around awhile. Many of the large and mid size investments have different levels of risk associated with them. It is possible to have a big variance in the growth area based on the type of segment of the industry the investment represents. Part of the reason for the variance is the type of equities focused on within the account. If you have an investment that is more technology based rather than an investment that is retail based then you should expect a more volatile ride.

I have seen many different values placed on companies to differentiate them from small to medium or medium to large capitalization. I like the value for small companies represented by any company worth less than one and a half billion dollars. Medium size companies are those that are worth between one and half billion and five billion. Large companies are those that are above five billion dollars.

One classic example has to do with Microsoft. When Bill Gates was a young, unknown technology geek, he offered a few investors the opportunity to help grow a business based on a computer he made in his garage; the risk of losing their money would have been huge. Here is a guy, a brilliant guy we know now, but then his only office was in his garage. He had an idea and needed a few dollars to get an idea off the ground. Once the idea began to take hold every investor had a chance to purchase shares of Microsoft, and those that did and held onto the shares watched the company grow from a small to medium to large company making them millions along the way!

Some growth investments could still be considered value, if they have been compared to others in their industry and are considered at a better value, then it can be a great choice. Many investors have defined value as purchasing equity at a better value because it has been beaten down due to some bad news or the overall market has taken the investment down to a point that is desired at its current valuation. This allows for value investments utilizing midsize and even small companies to be considered growth, but may have a less volatility since they have already been beaten down. However, many times a beaten down investment is on its way to zero, so you need to be careful. Many investments have defined their investments as value investment. However, it may be more aggressive in nature and the investment will be volatile because that is the nature of small and medium size investments.

It is important to find the fact sheets of the particular mutual funds found in your 401(k) choices, to see its exact philosophy for the investment. In order to do that, you may have to contact the administrator of the 401(k) plan to get a prospectus for each of the funds. The prospectus should also be available during the educational meetings held at a minimum of yearly.

5th Gear- Aggressive Growth Investments or Emerging Growth Investments

Aggressive growth investments are the highest risk of investments. The primary objective is to grow the portfolio without any attention to creating income. The investment will accomplish this by investing in securities considered to be aggressive growth in nature. Aggressive Growth investments can be made up of small, medium or large companies measured by their capitalization but are still emerging in their industry. Yet, most aggressive growth investments only deal in the small and medium size companies. Another

Some investments are specialty investments and may fit here as well. Specialty investments usually focus strongly on one category inside a category. As example, a technology investment may focus only on telecommunications, and would then be subject to the volatile moves of this individual segment, I would like to take you through a hypothetical illustration to help you understand variations of return. Imagine looking at a fact sheet of any investment you have put money into, and are looking to see your return. In 1999 the performance was 57%, however the following year in 2000 it has lost 17.8%, in 2001 it lost 12.2%, and in 2002 it lost 13.6%. Looking at the return and loss, you would say hey, I

can do the math, it would be 57% - 17.8% - 12.2% - 13.6% = +
14.6% but because the investment would compound the loss year
after year, you would have lost money. If you had invested around
twenty-eight thousand dollars on January 1, 1999 you would be
down around five hundred dollars after four years. Not too good!

Emerging Growth companies are often companies located in
emerging countries. Because of their international status, there are
extra risks associated with these investments. International
investments have risks associated to geo-political issues, exchange
rate risk on top of the market risk and economic risk all
investments can encounter. Why invest in higher risk portfolios?
In some cases their return of the portfolio can be much greater than
the return you can get in domestic investments.

Aggressive Growth investments often have an overall return
greater than those of the growth or growth and income
investments. However, the ride is not always straight up, and often
have a greater degree of volatility because of the massive swings
up and then down. I have seen aggressive growth investments in
1999 double their portfolios in the one year due to great returns
over one-hundred percent, only to lose all and even more of the
principal in the following years. That is why you should not place
all your eggs in this basket. Even knowing that the return over
time is better, you will be subject to emotional ups and downs
along the way. Also, when you are closer to retirement age, you

can't afford to lose a big percentage of your portfolio and wait for it to climb back.

Many aggressive investments are not worth your time, some are excellent, but the one key is to not allocate any more of the portfolio then 30% in aggressive growth investments and that is only true if you have more than ten years before retirement age.

Chapter 5

One financial advisors investment strategy

Understanding where you are going is the first question you need to ask.

Imagine sitting in front of a married couple who has been recommended to you from a current client, and they want financial advice helping them avoid mistakes they have seen others do in their retirement years. The couple has just recently decided to retire, and they have severed their employment so they can enjoy the rest of their life in comfort and looking forward to spending more time with each other and their grandkids. The problem is you have to deliver the news that if they keep living at their current level of spending, they will run out of money in less than fifteen years. Sound like fun! This is happening all the time, all across America. Why? Because most people, my estimate is 75% – 80% individuals do not know how much money they need to have available in order to give them the monthly income they need to live comfortably in retirement. It is sad when you go out to shop and you see an elderly person working, and you realize by their demeanor that they are working not because they enjoy the job, but because they have no other choice.

As we have learned that Americans are living longer, they require more money in retirement. If you add your financial income need each year you live in retirement and add in inflation so that you can keep pace with the cost of your living expenses, you would see a graph that every year grew needing more dollars then needed the previous year. If you can picture this uphill graph, you will realize it is the last few years that will cost the most, and these are often the years that the money will run out.

The first question you must ask yourself is simply, if you were to retire today, right now, how much income would you need for your everyday needs? Let's say you need five thousand a month, which is sixty thousand dollars a year. So what is your number?

The second question you need to ask yourself is what inflation number should you use? Why is this important? The inflation number has been about three percent over the last eighty-five years. However, if you go back and use the last sixty-year time frame then your inflation number would be four-and a half percent. Over the last ten years the inflation number has been less than that. So do you use 3%, 4%, or only 2%? This is important because this will regulate how much extra money you would need each year to add to your number.

The third important question you need to ask is at what age do you want to begin your retirement?
This question is important as it relates to the next question.

The fourth question is at what age do you want to use to show your life expectancy? This number as we have discussed earlier is one that seems to get larger every decade. Currently people are expected to live to the ripe ol' age of eighty-five. Some families have a tendency to have grandparents and or parents that have surpassed that number. Willard Scott, the weatherman that I remember seeing on the television news some twenty years ago, would share the picture and name of someone that has had a birthday that brought them to one hundred or beyond. So the importance of this number is very imprecise since I have still to find the person that knows the date that they will leave this life as we know it. Imagine you have placed the number ninety as the year for your demise, in reality you live to ninety-five. How much more money would you need? So much more than the first five years of your retirement because of the inflation and higher income need.

Now you begin to realize that you may want to be more conservative on this number and take the number that you will live to the age of one-hundred. So if you retire at the age of sixty-five and expect to live to one hundred, then you will need income for thirty-five years. Your nest egg will need to be much larger than if you lived only to eight-five and needed twenty years.

If you desire to retire earlier and begin your retirement when you turn sixty, then you need to add five more years, and this will make it a larger number you need.

One other note to help people understand another hard to understand issue retirement has on estimating the need. Every question I have asked up to know is based on the fact that you will live a long and healthy life in retirement. However, there are two possible other situations! One, being you die early. If this happens then from a monetary point, you will not drain the nest egg as you would if you lived a long healthy life. However, what if the third possibility happens, which is a long unhealthy life for you or your spouse. Not only would the numbers we have used be needed, but more dollars may be needed to support the medical bills necessary. All the retirement expenses you had planned for would still be needed, but you would need to spend money on health care, one of the most expensive cost on our resources. For help with this important number you can contact your financial advisor, however if your advisor has never had this conversation with you I need to ask what good are they?

How to research and allocate your investment choices found in your 401(k) plan

Items needed:

- One hour or less
- Your 401(k) investment choices (usually found on your quarterly statement, if not you may need to go online or contact your 401(k) administrator.
- The printouts of your mutual funds fact sheet found on the internet.
- The Retirement Plan Allocation Worksheet
- Your Personal Allocation Chart Worksheet
- The Investment Return Worksheet

First you need to fill out the Retirement Plan Allocation sheet to find your RQ and Temperament score by filling in your current age and your expected retirement age into the proper column. When you subtract your current age from your expected retirement age, you will have your RQ number. Take your RQ number and find the correct range to receive your score number. Place the score number into your personal allocation Chart worksheet and then you will need to determine your investor temperament.

Ask yourself this question, "how much volatility can I stomach?" Are you conservative, moderate, aggressive or somewhere in between in regard to your ability to handle volatility? Let's see if you are aggressive? Are you so aggressive that you can climb up a hill overlooking the ocean on a windy day; take out of your pocket all your money you own, and throw it into the air allowing the wind to blow it away for you to never hold again.

If you could do this and go home and still sleep like a baby, then yes you are able to consider yourself an aggressive investor. If on personal reflection, you could not do that but are willing to emotionally handle big swings in the stock market and be able to look at your financial investment statement every month and even though it has fallen forty percent in recent years, you still can sleep well, knowing by staying with your financial strategy, your portfolio will come back some day, then your temperament would be considered moderate aggressive.

If you are conservative but are willing to take some risk to get a little more gain then you can find on a certificate of deposit at the bank, then you are probably a conservative moderate temperament, and finally if you cannot stomach much loss in your portfolio consider yourself a conservative.

I need to take a moment and share one simple rule with you; it is called the rule of 72. This rule allows you to determine how many years it would take for you to double your money placed into an account with any rate of return. If you are getting a 6% return, then by dividing the 6 into 72 you would have 12 years. If your return was 9% then by dividing the 9 into 72 it would take 8 years to double your money. The rule of 72 is a mathematical concept and does not guarantee investment results or function as a predictor or how an investment will perform. It is an approximation of the impact of a targeted rate of return would have. Investments are subject to fluctuating returns and there is no assurance that any investment will double in value. Why is this important?

One of the biggest problems with Americans today is the lack of understanding what their retirement portfolio number needs to be to allow them the lifestyle they desire. Some would tell you that eighty percent of the working population has no idea of the amount of money they need invested on the day of their retirement to adequately investment their desired standard of living during the most sensitive years of their life. What I see happening is that many people retire because they reach a certain age, with little regard to knowing if they have enough money to support their retirement needs. Far too many generations of

Americans relied on the government or pensions, and did not have to think much about their income needs. However, today is different! There is little expectation that social security will survive forever, and pension plans are hard to find, so it is up to the individual. The real issue is that without knowing what the value of their portfolio needs to be on the day of retirement, and not knowing their date of death allowing them to know exactly how many years they need to have the portfolio last, most Americans are underfunded. Therefore, they needed to put more money away or get a better percentage gain on their invested money. Too many Americans have their portfolios so conservative that they will never be able to grow their retirement investments properly.

Taking no risk is taking the greatest risk of all! Why, because of a one word disaster, the word is inflation. Inflation will not allow you to have enough for retirement unless you can grow your portfolio more than you're losing with purchase power loss. Remember how the United States postage stamp seems to more than double every twenty years, if you do nothing more that make a few percentage points on your return, you will still be able to purchase less in the future. YOU MUST BEAT INFLATION AND TAXES to even hope to grow your account properly.

If you understand that you may need to have some risk in your portfolio, or you will not grow your portfolio enough. Having some risk does not mean you will fail, but allow more volatility into your portfolio usually means overall return.

Knowing about your goals and your own personality you need to determine your temperament score. When you have determined your temperament, follow the guide and place the percentage corresponding to your temperament into the income area of Your Personal Allocation Chart worksheet. Find the corresponding number from your RQ score and allocate from the bottom up until you run out of allocation. It's that easy!

Second, you need to get your 401(k) plan investment guide, it may be a statement or you may have to go online to your retirement plan homepage and sign in (often the password is your social security number or the last four numbers.) If, the social security number is not the correct password, then a plan administrator will need to give you your username and password, so this may not be available immediately.

Once you have the investment guide or statement in front of you, please find the section to lists all the investment choices you have available in your plan. Some people get confused and miss some of the choices, because the list is showing your current allocation. Make sure you have the list without the percentage allocation you are currently investing into. Once, you have the names of the investments available you need to go online to the fund family listed and get the performance of the fund outside your 401(k) and available to invest in any account. The reason for this extra step is simple; many of the investments in your 401(k) have a different start date from the 401(k) plan. Therefore the true history is often shorter if you use the 401(k) plan start date. Therefore it is important that you find the history of the fund outside the plan. At times the 401(k) plan has a name that is different than the actual investment outside the plan. This is why you may have to properly map the correct fund by calling the plan administrator and finding out the correct correlating investment.

When you have the list, you will need to first organize them into the proper categories, the categories are income, growth and income, growth, or aggressive growth. Take the Investment Return Worksheet, and enter each investment into the number column and then place it in the grid. If you have an investment that does not go back as many years as listed place a minus 2 in each answer. Investments that do not have a history can cause you untested and unneeded volatility. Take your fact sheet and place the returns from the fact sheet from each investment offered into the investment return category. After the investment returns have been entered, then subtract the investment return from the index return of the category and enter the results into the difference column.

Take the results and add or subtract the difference to get a rough estimate of how your fund under – or outperformed the index. Because this is not an accurate calculation method, I want to point out that this is meant to give you a guideline to understand how to compare the investment vehicles you have. This result will help you determine the quality of each of the investments offered in your 401(k) and should help you determine which investment has the best history.

5 important steps to weed out the good from bad

There are a few filters you may want to embrace in order to determine which investments you want to include or avoid. Having rules can help you save time, save money and possibly keep from making a mistake.

Rule #1 – Use Investments that have a track record.

This is your hard earned money, and you do not want to risk it on new products that have not been tested. I can remember early in my career when the firm I worked for would come out with a new mutual fund every month. It seemed we would call clients and let them know of the new opportunity, the great investment team they had choosing the investments inside the fund, and why we believed it to be good.

Over the years, I have learned that a new investment is just an untested investment, and even though the talent may be great, it still is new and usually has a different strategy that still makes it new.

I have used a fifteen year filter on most of my picks. Why, because there are more mutual funds than individual stocks available to the investor, I have heard it said many of the portfolio managers are under the age of thirty-five, and have only a few years of real investment experience. In order to avoid these issues, investing in an investment that has a longer track record could possibly help avoid mistakes made by so many other investors. But you need to make sure the portfolio managers have been the same over that time period. If the manager has less than ten years with the investment, then avoid it.

I remember in the 1990's and early 2000's that there was a new mutual fund being introduced to the market every month. The firm that represented the fund would tout the performance of the manager in another fund as a reason to buy this new investment. However, usually this new fund had a different investment style, and therefore would not have a track record. My simple rule is now to stay away from the new fund for awhile. Why, well there are more mutual funds then there are publicly traded stocks. I believe there are more than enough to choose from, so look for longer track records. One other note, make sure the lead manager has been part of the track record for a long time too. If you have a change in the lead manager, then it is probably a great time to get out.

There are a few exceptions to this rule. Some investments have closed themselves off from new investments once they become well funded. The reason is simple, mutual funds have to follow rules the investment management team has deemed worthy.

Similar to what we are discussing here! One rule is that no more than a certain percent of the whole portfolio amount can go into any one stock. This allows for diversification. As an example, if the rule stated only 4% can be in any one stock, this would allow a minimum of 25 different companies to be included. Another rule may be that the investment can only be up to 9% of the size of the company being invested into. This additional rule could limit the investment of a larger fund because they may want to invest the whole 4% from the first rule, but are not able to because the market capitalization on the investment will only allow a 2% investment. Some mutual funds will keep buying more and more companies as new money keeps pouring in and they are unable to add it to their earlier picks because of these filters. Thus, they have to look for newer companies to invest in. There will be a point where the investment managers will realize they have to compromise the quality of the picks to keep accepting new money, so to preserve the great performance of their mutual fund; they will close the doors to new investors.

Many believe that small company stocks have more risk associated because of their smaller size in regard to their capitalization. Middle capitalization stocks are less risky because they have done well enough to get passed the stigma of being the new kid on the block. Many have seen that once a company reaches middle capitalization status, their ride to becoming a large capitalization company may potentially happen much faster than it did to reach the middle point. Because many mid cap funds try to stay true to the middle capitalization concept, they will have to sell a stock when it does well, and look for new ones to replace. The choices are limited and they soon realize there are not enough quality stocks to choose from, so they close. Because of this you may want to shorten your filter on this segment or you may not get a good mid cap investment.

Rule #2 – Use Investments that have a team approach

How would you feel, knowing that you have only one pilot on your plane? For some that would not bother them, but I think most people would find comfort in knowing that there was a co-pilot and if the flight was international in nature maybe even another pilot available too. What if the manager died on the way to work, who would be looking after your investments? Maybe, the lead manager has a family emergency and needs be away for a few days, again who is functioning as your lead manager. Often a fund will employ managers for different areas of research and management. Maybe one manager deals with technology investments and another with financial positions. In either case having a team approach does have advantages.

Rule #3 – Use Investments that have a lower ongoing expense structure

One factor in performance or lack of performance can be found in the fact that mutual funds have ongoing expenses. I have found that many people do not fully understand the fees being charged inside a mutual fund, and when I say many people, I am including most financial advisors. Most individuals know that it cost money to run any business. Money to pay for employees, the utilities to keep the lights on, cost related to marketing, and printing costs as well as expenses related to their function of service. For mutual funds, they have to pay all the managers and all the people necessary to provide for the function of the funds existence. The funds have cost related to printing material for distribution to shareholders and potential investors to inform and keep all compliance in check. Also, there are costs involved with paying the financial advisors, and finally costs involved in the actual trading for the fund.

Most of the costs can be budgeted and projected and these fees are listed in the fund prospectus. The ongoing fees and expenses are those that are projected but not using the unknown costs like trading costs. Therefore, the expense ongoing is not accurate but a prediction of fixed expenses. If you realize this, then you know that the actual number is used. Most funds will not even share their cost and expenses from the previous year. This is not a transparent policy. Often you can ask for a supplemental prospectus, but again most advisors don't even know one exist, and they believe the number in the prospectus is accurate. Sad, but true!

I have heard it stated that the average fund fee mentioned in the prospectus is 1.4% annually depending on the type of fund. But when you tack on the trading and other miscellaneous fees, it often can go up to over 2%, with some more aggressive funds over 3%. Now I don't mind paying for service, but I do believe most of us would like to know the real costs. The performance numbers used in mutual fund facts sheets and on the internet are the returns after these expenses have been taken, so your actual performance would have been higher but they needed to be paid.

Knowing your fee structure can help you potentially get higher return, mainly if you have a similar investment with similar performance then; it stands to reason if you choose the investment with lower expenses, you may squeeze out an additional return percentage annually. If you are able to produce a little extra return every year because you are saving on the internal expenses then you may get a little extra allocation of income when you need it later in your retirement years.

Rule #4 – Use Investments that get most of the upside of the market

Performance return is what every investor is after, and yet we know if your performance outpaces the overall market, then you also have the potential of underperforming the entire market. For years, money managers were paid to get performance, until someone finally realized that by taking on risk to get good returns, also meant that the extra risk will come back and bite you when the markets are not so hot!

One key point I need to make on comparing your return to the overall market return. The Dow Jones Industrial Average that is talked about every day on every news channel is not the index to use! When did thirty large cap companies all in the industrial sector become a beacon for the whole economy? Thirty stocks to represent the thousands that are out there. The Dow Jones is up; the Dow Jones is down, so what! It is like saying that thirty high school seniors all from the same zip code took the SAT test, and based on these thirty test results, we have enough information to make a statement about the educational knowledge of the whole nation of senior high seniors.

When I was in high school, we had an excellent math program that our principal was so proud he went to the local junior college principal and asked for a teacher to come and teach calculus to his students. For a few years this high school principal would bug the junior college principal about the opportunity, but the junior college principal thought that there was no way high school students could handle a course most college students struggled in. So to get the principal off his back, he agreed to administer a test to the students. The principal had set up thirty students from his school and thirty from a rival high school to take the test. When the scores came in, twenty-seven of the students from our high school passed, and three from the rival school did too. The junior college principal was so impressed the first year he came and taught the class at the high school. My point is simply when one school had over a 90% pass rate the other school had less than 10%. Neither school would be an accurate measure on the ability of high school students to take a calculus math class. Yet, this is the measure that is used every day to try to get the average person excited about the stock market. Yikes!

Use the correct index to compare your performance, and try to avoid using the Dow Jones general index as a measuring stick. The S & P 500 has five hundred companies representing all different industries to represent the economy. Where there are so many different index's to choose from, I still think the S & P 500 is the better index for the average person to compare equity returns to.

My rule is simple, when the market is up, you should get at least 75% of the upside. That means if the S + P 500 is up 20% in a given year, your return needs to be at least 15%. Not hard to measure. But this is only half the equation needed. This rule is only effective if rule #5 is used in conjunction with rule #4.

Rule #5 – Use Investments that protects against the downside of the market

Having a money manager that knows how to balance risk with reward is very important. So measuring the down side of a investment is just as important as measuring the upside of a investment. I remember back in early 2000, when I was taking to an investor about a balanced portfolio, and how his portfolio was anything but balanced. He had received a huge percentage gain the year before, and was feeling like investing for growth was easy. I recommended a portfolio that had an average return that represented more like the average returns in the market over the last seventy-five years. He looked at me and simply asked "Do I look stupid to you?" I have gotten over 75% return last year and if I listen to you I would only have around 20% return. I remember saying, "no if you listen to me, you probably will have about half that." I could not convince this investor to take my advice with the truth. However, a year later, this investor called me and said he had stupid written on his forehead and asked if I can help him reallocate.

When investing in the stock market, it is not only possible, but recommended to get a more consistent return, then to get huge swings in your portfolio. What good is it to make a huge return, only to lose it all the next year!

My rule for protecting the portfolio is to find investments that lose only about half of what the overall market has lost. If the S + P 500 loses 20% in a given year, your return should be down around 10%. If you combine this with rule #4, then you could possibly outpace the overall market over a market rotation.

Knowing when to slow down your investment vehicle!

How often have you heard the comment from financial professionals, that you need to have a good portfolio, properly diversified and then to stick to your guns and not to make a change very often. The buy and hold approach has been preached from financial street corners for decades. However, there are times when I believe you as an investor need to have a proactive approach to protecting your investments.

When driving your car, there are times you need to simply stop the car and park it whether it is because you need to rest, or the car is in need of a rest. **I want to make one comment very clear!** I am not advocating market timing as an approach to trying to outperform the market, only a time to rest the investments from a possible catastrophic event.

When there is an event in our world that is an obvious and rattling event, then you want to pull your investments over and put them in a safer allocation for a time. One event was when America was attacked on 9/11 by terrorist. We all remember the images of the two towers were struck by airplanes and the utter devastation that followed. This is one of those times that would have made a difference to place your portfolio on hold. Another time, was when America had sent war ships to Iraq. An action that seemed to signal a coming confrontation. Why else would we be sending ships! The beginning of the credit melt-down would be another good time to slow down your vehicle, and as it turned out, was a good time to completely stop the vehicle and get out.

Terrorist attacks are all awful, because people are losing their lives. The roadside bombs or suicide bombers are bad, but not on the scale I am talking about. The events I am suggesting you take an action on are big enough to cause concern that the markets will behave predictably bad for a time. So, use your common sense and slow it down or stop it all together.

How you do this is simple! You find the one money market fund in the choices you are given, and find a Government bond investment and a corporate bond investment. To slow down the investments place a third into each of these three investments. If you are truly scared by the volatility of the markets like with what happened with the credit melt down in 2008', then place all your investments in the money market. This is not an investment strategy you are going to employ for a long period of time. Remember, we need to grow the portfolio over inflation over time. However, this is meant to keep your portfolio from falling down in a hole when it seems the whole market, because of a big ugly event, can really hurt your performance. If you fall less than the overall market, then it will be easier for you to get back out of the hole, since you are closer to the top then if you stayed in the same buy and hold allocation you began with.

The other part of this equation is when to get back in to growing the market. I would recommend common sense again, and not let your emotions get the best of you. When the Iraq war was going on and the American troops pulled down the statue of Sodom Hussain, that was my signal. When the credit market crunch happened, it was seeing actions being taken by the Federal Reserve, and giving them a few months, so even though it was early, putting money back into play by December of the same year may have been a good opportunity. Of course the markets did not get going for another few months, but we don't have the crystal ball to know the exact time. This is not meant as a timing devise to allow our emotions to rule, just common sense to keep from falling hard.

Chapter 6   Putting it all together

The steps to complete your 401(k) evaluation is as follows:

⟹   Read this manual

⟹   Collect the 401(k) information from your employer. Mainly what you want is the choices list from the retirement plan.

⟹   Evaluate the choices by using the investment surveyor after you have determined if the investment is an income investment, a growth and income investment, a growth investment, or an aggressive growth investment.

⟹   After finding a choice for each of the investments, fill out the Retirement Plan Allocation Sheet. Have your RQ score and your bond percentage ready.

⟹   Fill out Your Personal Allocation Chart by using the RQ score and your bond percentage to find a proper allocation to use during most the year.

⊃⟹   Make a list of the government bond investments, corporate bond investments, and money market investments for when troubled time arise, and you need to put your investments into a lower risk due to world tensions.

⊃⟹   Use Your Personal Allocation Chart, use the investments that the Investment Surveyor scored, and put in the proper percentage toward retirement investments.

Alright young padawon' I have given you a beginner education on investing. It is time for you to do it! Just remember, it is about you taking control over you future and not handing it over to your Government, your employer, or even your financial advisor. In all cases, it is you who will be required to live with the results.

Most people do not have much financial education, and therefore just stick their head in the sand when it comes to making decisions on finance. You can't afford to take this approach any longer. Fear of making a mistake is not a good enough reason to have your future ruined by lack of money. Though, even by doing everything as well as possible will not ensure enough money for you, only give you a much better chance at having the retirement you deserve!

Go forward, make up your mind to take the bull by the horns and take your future in your hands.

If you find yourself making much better decisions regarding the returns and learning how to protect your returns in your retirement portfolio, then let me know. We all love to hear that effort in helping another person is appreciated! Let me know by sending an email to jimhayne@gmail.com.

The Retirement Worksheets

The Retirement Plan Allocation Sheet

Your Personal Allocation Chart

Income Comparison Chart 4 Copies

Growth and Income Comparison Chart 4 Copies

Growth Comparison Chart 4 Copies

Aggressive Growth Comparison Chart 4 Copies

Retirement Plan Allocation Sheet

Name of Participant: ____Sample Sheet - 41 Year Old Mod/Aggressive John Nobody______

The first step is to find your RQ number.

1. At what age do you desire to retire

    _65__ RA

2. What is your current age

    -    _41__ CA

    Subtract your current age from your desired retirement age

    =   _24__ RQ

If your RQ number falls between 50 – 25 years = you receive a score of 5

If your RQ number falls between 11 – 25 years = you receive a score of 6

If your RQ number falls between 5 – 10 years = you receive a score of 7

If your RQ number falls between 0 – 5 years = you receive a score

The second step is to understand your Investing Temperament.

Circle the one temperament that matches yours ability to emotionally handle the ups and downs of the stock market. For instance, if you begin losing sleep over a downturn in the stock market you would be considered conservative. If however, you can take huge swings in the stock market and feel comfortable losing 40% -50% in one year, you would be aggressive.

Conservative   Moderate   Moderate/Aggressive   Aggressive

Conservative = 50%

Moderate   = 30%

Mod/Agr   = 20%

Aggressive   = 10%

The percentage listed above represents the amount of your entire portfolio that should be invested into the bond area of your investments.

Now take the percentage from the list above that matches your investing temperament and place the number in the bond investment area, on the chart on the following page.

Retirement Plan Allocation Sheet

Name of Participant: ____

The first step is to find your RQ number.

1. At what age do you desire to retire

    ______ RA

2. What is your current age

    - ______ CA

   Subtract your current age from your desired retirement age

    = ______ RQ

If your RQ number falls between 50 – 25 years   =   you receive a score of 5

If your RQ number falls between 11 – 25 years   =   you receive a score of 6

If your RQ number falls between 5 – 10 years   =   you receive a score of 7

If your RQ number falls between 0 – 5 years   =   you receive a score of 8

What Is Your RQ Score?   ________________

The second step is to understand your Investing Temperament.

Circle the one temperament that matches yours ability to emotionally handle the ups and downs of the stock market. For instance, if you begin losing sleep over a downturn in the stock market you would be considered conservative. If however, you can take huge swings in the stock market and feel comfortable losing 40% -50% in one year, you would be aggressive.

Conservative   Moderate   Moderate/Aggressive   Aggressive

Conservative = 50%

Moderate   = 30%

Mod/Agr   = 20%

Aggressive   = 10%

The percentage listed above represents the amount of your entire portfolio that should be invested into the bond area of your investments.

Now take the percentage from the list above that matches your investing temperament and place the number in the bond investment area, on the chart on the following page.

What Is Your Investing Temperament? ___________

Sample

You're personal Allocation Chart

Begin by placing the percentage of bond investments into the allocation chart below from your temperament score. Then use your RQ number to multiply by the number in Growth and Income investment box. If your number is greater than the percent you 9(have left, that's your allocation! If you have any percentage left over then multiplies your RQ number by the number in the Growth investments box. Whatever is left over; place in the Aggressive investment box. When you know your percentage, find the investments that fit the criteria of that category and place them in the appropriate box.   Pretty simple once you get the hang of it!

Conservative Investor With RQ of 6:

50% in Bond Investments

Take Highest Percentage In Next More Aggressive Allocation And Multiply By Your RQ Score

Bond Investment Percentage: (10% - 50%)   50%

Growth and Income Percentage: Multiplier is 8

(8 x 6 = 36 %)   40%

Growth Percentage: Multiplier is 6

(6 x 6 = 36%) Only 14% Percent Is Left So We Place   14%

Aggressive Growth Percentage 0% - 20%

Since There Is No Percentage Left It Will Remain 0%   0%

Sample

You're personal Allocation Chart

Begin by placing the percentage of bond investments into the allocation chart below from your temperament score. Then use your RQ number to multiply by the number in Growth and Income investment box. If your number is greater than the percent you 9(have left, that's your allocation! If you have any percentage left over then multiplies your RQ number by the number in the Growth investments box. Whatever is left over; place in the Aggressive investment box. When you know your percentage, find the investments that fit the criteria of that category and place them in the appropriate box.   Pretty simple once you get the hang of it!

Aggressive Investor With RQ of 5:

10% in Bond Investments

Take Highest Percentage In Next More Aggressive Allocation And Multiply By Your RQ Score

Bond Investment Percentage: (10% - 50%)   10%

Growth and Income Percentage: Multiplier is 8

(8 x 5 = 40 %)   40%

Growth Percentage: Multiplier is 6

(6 x5 = 30%)   30%

Aggressive Growth Percentage 0% - 20%

Remainder is 20%   20%

You're personal Allocation

The first step is to find your RQ number.

1. At what age do you desire to retire

    _______ RA

2. What is your current age

    -    _______ CA

    Subtract your current age from your desired retirement age

    =   _______ RQ

If your RQ number falls between 50 – 25 years   =   you
receive a score of 5

If your RQ number falls between 11 – 25 years   =   you
receive a score of 6

If your RQ number falls between 5 – 10 years   =   you
receive a score of 7

If your RQ number falls between 0 – 5 years   =   you
receive a score of 8

What Is Your RQ Score?   _________________

The second step is to understand your Investing Temperament.

Circle the one temperament that matches yours ability to emotionally handle the ups and downs of the stock market. For instance, if you begin losing sleep over a downturn in the stock market you would be considered conservative. If however, you can take huge swings in the stock market and feel comfortable losing 40% -50% in one year, you would be aggressive.

Conservative   Moderate   Moderate/Aggressive   Aggressive

Conservative = 50%

Moderate   = 30%

Mod/Agr   = 20%

Aggressive   = 10%

The percentage listed above represents the amount of your entire portfolio that should be invested into the bond area of your investments.

Now take the percentage from the list above that matches your investing temperament and place the number in the bond investment area, on the chart on the following page.

What Is Your Investing Temperament? ____________

Your Personal Investment Allocation

RQ Score = _______

Investment Temperament _________

Bond Allocation _______

Growth + Income
8 x RQ Score _________

Growth
6 x RQ Score _________

Aggressive Growth
Left Over Amount _________

Income Investment Comparison Chart

Example: If in your 401(k) you had a choice of ABNFX, this is how to compare to the index to see actual returns over time.

Year	Barclays US Agg.	Bond Fund (ABNFX)	Difference
2000	11.63%	6.2%	-5.43%
2001	8.44%	7.2%	-1.24%
2002	10.25%	6.1%	-4.15%
2003	4.10%	12.2%	+8.1%
2004	4.34%	5.8%	+1.46%
2005	2.43%	1.9%	-.53%
2006	4.33%	5.9%	+1.57%
2007	6.97%	3.4%	-3.57%
2008	5.24	-12.2%	-15.44%
2009	5.93%	14.9%	+8.97%
2010	6.54%	7.3%	+.76%
2011	7.84%	6.5%	-1.34%
2012	4.21%	5.9%	+1.69%
2013	-2.02%	-2.0%	+.02%
2014	5.97%	5.5%	-.47%
2015	0.55%	.20%	-0.45%
2016	2.65%	2.70%	+.05%
2017	3.54%	3.47%	-.07%
2018	0.01%	0.14%	+.13%

Income Investment Comparison Chart

Fund From 401(K) You Are Comparing: _______________________

Year	Barclays US Agg.	Your Fund ________	Difference
2000	11.63%	________	________
2001	8.44%	________	________
2002	10.25%	________	________
2003	4.10%	________	________
2004	4.34%	________	________
2005	2.43%	________	________
2006	4.33%	________	________
2007	6.97%	________	________
2008	5.24	________	________
2009	5.93%	________	________
2010	6.54%	________	________
2011	7.84%	________	________
2012	4.21%	________	________
2013	-2.02%	________	________
2014	5.97%	________	________
2015	0.55%	________	________
2016	2.65%	________	________
2017	3.54%	________	________
2018	0.01%	________	________

Take your fund returns and subtract from Barclays US Agg. Returns

Total Difference= If your investment does not have a ten year history, then use 2%

<u>Barclays US AGG Index Annualized Return as of 6-30-2019</u>

1 year = 7.87%   3 year = 2.31%   5 year = 2.95%   10 year = 2.90%

The performance data quoted represents past performance. Past performance is not a guarantee of future results. Indices are unmanaged and cannot be invested into directly.

Income Investment Comparison Chart

Fund From 401(K) You Are Comparing: _______________________

Year	Barclays US Agg.	Your Fund _______	Difference
2000	11.63%	_______	_______
2001	8.44%	_______	_______
2002	10.25%	_______	_______
2003	4.10%	_______	_______
2004	4.34%	_______	_______
2005	2.43%	_______	_______
2006	4.33%	_______	_______
2007	6.97%	_______	_______
2008	5.24	_______	_______
2009	5.93%	_______	_______
2010	6.54%	_______	_______
2011	7.84%	_______	_______
2012	4.21%	_______	_______
2013	-2.02%	_______	_______
2014	5.97%	_______	_______
2015	0.55%	_______	_______
2016	2.65%	_______	_______
2017	3.54%	_______	_______
2018	0.01%	_______	_______

Take your fund returns and subtract from Barclays US Agg. Returns

Total Difference= If your investment does not have a ten year history, then use 2%

Barclays US AGG Index Annualized Return as of 6-30-2019

1 year = 7.87%   3 year = 2.31%   5 year = 2.95%   10 year = 2.90%

The performance data quoted represents past performance. Past performance is not a guarantee of future results. Indices are unmanaged and cannot be invested into directly.

Income Investment Comparison Chart

Fund From 401(K) You Are Comparing: ______________________

Year	Barclays US Agg.	Your Fund ________	Difference
2000	11.63%	________	________
2001	8.44%	________	________
2002	10.25%	________	________
2003	4.10%	________	________
2004	4.34%	________	________
2005	2.43%	________	________
2006	4.33%	________	________
2007	6.97%	________	________
2008	5.24	________	________
2009	5.93%	________	________
2010	6.54%	________	________
2011	7.84%	________	________
2012	4.21%	________	________
2013	-2.02%	________	________
2014	5.97%	________	________
2015	0.55%	________	________
2016	2.65%	________	________
2017	3.54%	________	________
2018	0.01%	________	________

	Take your fund returns and subtract from Barclays US Agg. Returns	Total Difference= If your investment does not have a ten year history, then use 2%

Barclays US AGG Index Annualized Return as of 6-30-2019

1 year = 7.87%   3 year = 2.31%   5 year = 2.95%   10 year = 2.90%

The performance data quoted represents past performance. Past performance is not a guarantee of future results. Indices are unmanaged and cannot be invested into directly.

Income Investment Comparison Chart

Fund From 401(K) You Are Comparing: _______________________

Year	Barclays US Agg.	Your Fund ________	Difference
2000	11.63%	________	________
2001	8.44%	________	________
2002	10.25%	________	________
2003	4.10%	________	________
2004	4.34%	________	________
2005	2.43%	________	________
2006	4.33%	________	________
2007	6.97%	________	________
2008	5.24	________	________
2009	5.93%	________	________
2010	6.54%	________	________
2011	7.84%	________	________
2012	4.21%	________	________
2013	-2.02%	________	________
2014	5.97%	________	________
2015	0.55%	________	________
2016	2.65%	________	________
2017	3.54%	________	________
2018	0.01%	________	________

Take your fund returns and subtract from Barclays US Agg. Returns

Total Difference=
If your investment does not have a ten year history, then use 2%

Barclays US AGG Index Annualized Return as of 6-30-2019

1 year = 7.87%   3 year = 2.31%   5 year = 2.95%   10 year = 2.90%

The performance data quoted represents past performance. Past performance is not a guarantee of future results. Indices are unmanaged and cannot be invested into directly.

Growth and Income Comparison Chart

Fund From 401(K) You Are Comparing: _______________________

Year	Russell 1000 Value	Your Fund	Difference
2000	7.01%	_______	_______
2001	-5.59%	_______	_______
2002	-15.52%	_______	_______
2003	30.03%	_______	_______
2004	16.49%	_______	_______
2005	7.05%	_______	_______
2006	22.25%	_______	_______
2007	-0.17%	_______	_______
2008	-36.85	_______	_______
2009	19.69%	_______	_______
2010	15.51%	_______	_______
2011	0.39%	_______	_______
2012	17.51%	_______	_______
2013	32.53%	_______	_______
2014	13.45%	_______	_______
2015	-3.83%	_______	_______
2016	17.34%	_______	_______
2017	13.66%	_______	_______
2018	-8.27%	_______	_______

Take your fund returns and subtract from Russell 1000 Value Returns

Total Difference=
If your investment does not have a ten year history, then use 7%

Russell 1000 Value Index Annualized Return as of 6-30-2019

1 year = 8.46%   3 year = 10.19%   5 year = 7.46%   10 year = 13.19%

The performance data quoted represents past performance. Past performance is not a guarantee of future results. Indices are unmanaged and cannot be invested into directly.

Growth and Income Comparison Chart

Fund From 401(K) You Are Comparing: _______________________

Year	Russell 1000 Value	Your Fund	Difference
2000	7.01%	______	______
2001	-5.59%	______	______
2002	-15.52%	______	______
2003	30.03%	______	______
2004	16.49%	______	______
2005	7.05%	______	______
2006	22.25%	______	______
2007	-0.17%	______	______
2008	-36.85	______	______
2009	19.69%	______	______
2010	15.51%	______	______
2011	0.39%	______	______
2012	17.51%	______	______
2013	32.53%	______	______
2014	13.45%	______	______
2015	-3.83%	______	______
2016	17.34%	______	______
2017	13.66%	______	______
2018	-8.27%	______	______

Take your fund returns and subtract from Russell 1000 Value Returns

Total Difference=
If your investment does not have a ten year history, then use 7%

Russell 1000 Value Index Annualized Return as of 6-30-2019

1 year = 8.46%   3 year = 10.19%   5 year = 7.46%   10 year = 13.19%

The performance data quoted represents past performance. Past performance is not a guarantee of future results. Indices are unmanaged and cannot be invested into directly.

Growth and Income Comparison Chart

Fund From 401(K) You Are Comparing: _______________________

Year	Russell 1000 Value	Your Fund	Difference
2000	7.01%	_______	_______
2001	-5.59%	_______	_______
2002	-15.52%	_______	_______
2003	30.03%	_______	_______
2004	16.49%	_______	_______
2005	7.05%	_______	_______
2006	22.25%	_______	_______
2007	-0.17%	_______	_______
2008	-36.85	_______	_______
2009	19.69%	_______	_______
2010	15.51%	_______	_______
2011	0.39%	_______	_______
2012	17.51%	_______	_______
2013	32.53%	_______	_______
2014	13.45%	_______	_______
2015	-3.83%	_______	_______
2016	17.34%	_______	_______
2017	13.66%	_______	_______
2018	-8.27%	_______	_______

Take your fund returns and subtract from Russell 1000 Value Returns

Total Difference=
If your investment does not have a ten year history, then use 7%

Russell 1000 Value Index Annualized Return as of 6-30-2019

1 year = 8.46%   3 year = 10.19%   5 year = 7.46%   10 year = 13.19%

The performance data quoted represents past performance. Past performance is not a guarantee of future results. Indices are unmanaged and cannot be invested into directly.

Growth and Income Comparison Chart

Fund From 401(K) You Are Comparing: _______________________

Year	Russell 1000 Value	Your Fund	Difference
2000	7.01%	_______	_______
2001	-5.59%	_______	_______
2002	-15.52%	_______	_______
2003	30.03%	_______	_______
2004	16.49%	_______	_______
2005	7.05%	_______	_______
2006	22.25%	_______	_______
2007	-0.17%	_______	_______
2008	-36.85	_______	_______
2009	19.69%	_______	_______
2010	15.51%	_______	_______
2011	0.39%	_______	_______
2012	17.51%	_______	_______
2013	32.53%	_______	_______
2014	13.45%	_______	_______
2015	-3.83%	_______	_______
2016	17.34%	_______	_______
2017	13.66%	_______	_______
2018	-8.27%	_______	_______

	Take your fund returns and subtract from Russell 1000 Value Returns	Total Difference= If your investment does not have a ten year history, then use 7%

Russell 1000 Value Index Annualized Return as of 6-30-2019

1 year = 8.46%   3 year = 10.19%   5 year = 7.46%   10 year = 13.19%

The performance data quoted represents past performance. Past performance is not a guarantee of future results. Indices are unmanaged and cannot be invested into directly.

Growth Investment Comparison Chart

Fund From 401(K) You Are Comparing: _______________________

Year	S + P 500 Index	Your Fund	Difference
2000	-10.14%	_______	_______
2001	-13.04%	_______	_______
2002	-23.37%	_______	_______
2003	26.38%	_______	_______
2004	8.99%	_______	_______
2005	3.00%	_______	_______
2006	13.62%	_______	_______
2007	3.53%	_______	_______
2008	-38.49%	_______	_______
2009	23.45%	_______	_______
2010	12.78%	_______	_______
2011	0.00%	_______	_______
2012	13.41%	_______	_______
2013	29.60%	_______	_______
2014	11.39%	_______	_______
2015	-0.73%	_______	_______
2016	9.54%	_______	_______
2017	19.42%	_______	_______
2018	-6.24%	_______	_______

Take your fund returns and subtract from S+P 500 returns

Total Difference=
If your investment does not have a ten year history, then use 7%

S + P 500 Index Annualized Return as of 7-31-2019

1 year = 7.99%   3 year = 13.36%   5 year = 11.34%   10 year = 14.03%

The performance data quoted represents past performance. Past performance is not a guarantee of future results. Indices are unmanaged and cannot be invested into directly.

Growth Investment Comparison Chart

Fund From 401(K) You Are Comparing: _______________________

Year	S + P 500 Index	Your Fund	Difference
2000	-10.14%	_______	_______
2001	-13.04%	_______	_______
2002	-23.37%	_______	_______
2003	26.38%	_______	_______
2004	8.99%	_______	_______
2005	3.00%	_______	_______
2006	13.62%	_______	_______
2007	3.53%	_______	_______
2008	-38.49%	_______	_______
2009	23.45%	_______	_______
2010	12.78%	_______	_______
2011	0.00%	_______	_______
2012	13.41%	_______	_______
2013	29.60%	_______	_______
2014	11.39%	_______	_______
2015	-0.73%	_______	_______
2016	9.54%	_______	_______
2017	19.42%	_______	_______
2018	-6.24%	_______	_______

Take your fund returns and subtract from S+P 500 returns

Total Difference=
If your investment does not have a ten year history, then use 7%

S + P 500 Index Annualized Return as of 7-31-2019

1 year = 7.99%   3 year = 13.36%   5 year = 11.34%   10 year = 14.03%

The performance data quoted represents past performance. Past performance is not a guarantee of future results. Indices are unmanaged and cannot be invested into directly.

Growth Investment Comparison Chart

Fund From 401(K) You Are Comparing: _______________________

Year	S + P 500 Index	Your Fund	Difference
2000	-10.14%	_______	_______
2001	-13.04%	_______	_______
2002	-23.37%	_______	_______
2003	26.38%	_______	_______
2004	8.99%	_______	_______
2005	3.00%	_______	_______
2006	13.62%	_______	_______
2007	3.53%	_______	_______
2008	-38.49%	_______	_______
2009	23.45%	_______	_______
2010	12.78%	_______	_______
2011	0.00%	_______	_______
2012	13.41%	_______	_______
2013	29.60%	_______	_______
2014	11.39%	_______	_______
2015	-0.73%	_______	_______
2016	9.54%	_______	_______
2017	19.42%	_______	_______
2018	-6.24%	_______	_______
		Take your fund returns and subtract from S+P 500 returns	Total Difference= If your investment does not have a ten year history, then use 7%

S + P 500 Index Annualized Return as of 7-31-2019

1 year = 7.99%   3 year = 13.36%   5 year = 11.34%   10 year = 14.03%

The performance data quoted represents past performance. Past performance is not a guarantee of future results. Indices are unmanaged and cannot be invested into directly.

Growth Investment Comparison Chart

Fund From 401(K) You Are Comparing: ___________________

Year	S + P 500 Index	Your Fund	Difference
2000	-10.14%	_______	_______
2001	-13.04%	_______	_______
2002	-23.37%	_______	_______
2003	26.38%	_______	_______
2004	8.99%	_______	_______
2005	3.00%	_______	_______
2006	13.62%	_______	_______
2007	3.53%	_______	_______
2008	-38.49%	_______	_______
2009	23.45%	_______	_______
2010	12.78%	_______	_______
2011	0.00%	_______	_______
2012	13.41%	_______	_______
2013	29.60%	_______	_______
2014	11.39%	_______	_______
2015	-0.73%	_______	_______
2016	9.54%	_______	_______
2017	19.42%	_______	_______
2018	-6.24%	_______	_______

Take your fund returns and subtract from S+P 500 returns

Total Difference= If your investment does not have a ten year history, then use 7%

S + P 500 Index Annualized Return as of 7-31-2019

1 year = 7.99%   3 year = 13.36%   5 year = 11.34%   10 year = 14.03%

The performance data quoted represents past performance. Past performance is not a guarantee of future results. Indices are unmanaged and cannot be invested into directly.

Aggressive Growth Comparison Chart

Year	Russell 2000 Growth	Your Fund	Difference
2000	-22.43%	_______	_______
2001	-9.23%	_______	_______
2002	-30.26%	_______	_______
2003	48.54%	_______	_______
2004	14.31%	_______	_______
2005	4.15%	_______	_______
2006	13.35%	_______	_______
2007	7.05%	_______	_______
2008	-38.54%	_______	_______
2009	34.47%	_______	_______
2010	29.09%	_______	_______
2011	-2.91%	_______	_______
2012	14.59%	_______	_______
2013	43.30%	_______	_______
2014	5.6%	_______	_______
2015	-1.38%	_______	_______
2016	11.32%	_______	_______
2017	22.17%	_______	_______
2018	-9.31%	_______	_______

Take your fund returns and subtract from S+P 500 returns

Total Difference=
If your investment does not have a ten year history, then use 7%

Russell 2000 Growth Index Annualized Return as of 6-30-2019

1 year = -.0.49%   3 year = 14.69%   5 year = 8.63%   10 year = 14.41%

The performance data quoted represents past performance. Past performance is not a guarantee of future results. Indices are unmanaged and cannot be invested into directly.

Aggressive Growth Comparison Chart

Year	Russell 2000 Growth	Your Fund	Difference
2000	-22.43%	_______	_______
2001	-9.23%	_______	_______
2002	-30.26%	_______	_______
2003	48.54%	_______	_______
2004	14.31%	_______	_______
2005	4.15%	_______	_______
2006	13.35%	_______	_______
2007	7.05%	_______	_______
2008	-38.54%	_______	_______
2009	34.47%	_______	_______
2010	29.09%	_______	_______
2011	-2.91%	_______	_______
2012	14.59%	_______	_______
2013	43.30%	_______	_______
2014	5.6%	_______	_______
2015	-1.38%	_______	_______
2016	11.32%	_______	_______
2017	22.17%	_______	_______
2018	-9.31%	_______	_______

Take your fund returns and subtract from S+P 500 returns

Total Difference=
If your investment does not have a ten year history, then use 7%

Russell 2000 Growth Index Annualized Return as of 6-30-2019

1 year = -.0.49%   3 year = 14.69%   5 year = 8.63%   10 year = 14.41%

The performance data quoted represents past performance. Past performance is not a guarantee of future results. Indices are unmanaged and cannot be invested into directly.

Aggressive Growth Comparison Chart

Year	Russell 2000 Growth	Your Fund	Difference
2000	-22.43%	_________	_________
2001	-9.23%	_________	_________
2002	-30.26%	_________	_________
2003	48.54%	_________	_________
2004	14.31%	_________	_________
2005	4.15%	_________	_________
2006	13.35%	_________	_________
2007	7.05%	_________	_________
2008	-38.54%	_________	_________
2009	34.47%	_________	_________
2010	29.09%	_________	_________
2011	-2.91%	_________	_________
2012	14.59%	_________	_________
2013	43.30%	_________	_________
2014	5.6%	_________	_________
2015	-1.38%	_________	_________
2016	11.32%	_________	_________
2017	22.17%	_________	_________
2018	-9.31%	_________	_________

Take your fund returns and subtract from S+P 500 returns

Total Difference=
If your investment does not have a ten year history, then use 7%

<u>Russell 2000 Growth Index Annualized Return as of 6-30-2019</u>

1 year = -.0.49%   3 year = 14.69%   5 year = 8.63%   10 year = 14.41%

The performance data quoted represents past performance. Past performance is not a guarantee of future results. Indices are unmanaged and cannot be invested into directly.

Aggressive Growth Comparison Chart

Year	Russell 2000 Growth	Your Fund	Difference
2000	-22.43%	_______	_______
2001	-9.23%	_______	_______
2002	-30.26%	_______	_______
2003	48.54%	_______	_______
2004	14.31%	_______	_______
2005	4.15%	_______	_______
2006	13.35%	_______	_______
2007	7.05%	_______	_______
2008	-38.54%	_______	_______
2009	34.47%	_______	_______
2010	29.09%	_______	_______
2011	-2.91%	_______	_______
2012	14.59%	_______	_______
2013	43.30%	_______	_______
2014	5.6%	_______	_______
2015	-1.38%	_______	_______
2016	11.32%	_______	_______
2017	22.17%	_______	_______
2018	-9.31%	_______	_______
		Take your fund returns and subtract from S+P 500 returns	Total Difference= If your investment does not have a ten year history, then use 7%

<u>Russell 2000 Growth Index Annualized Return as of 6-30-2019</u>

1 year = -.0.49%   3 year = 14.69%   5 year = 8.63%   10 year = 14.41%

The performance data quoted represents past performance. Past performance is not a guarantee of future results. Indices are unmanaged and cannot be invested into directly.

Your Final Allocation Based On Sub Accounts You Like In Your 401(k) Account. You May Have Found Two Or Three In The Same Category (Bond, Growth and Income, Growth, Aggressive Growth) And Want To Diversify Into Those. I Have Included Three Slots, or Possible Investment Choices For Each Category.

Your Final 401 (k) Allocation

Bond Allocation _____%

1.
2.
3.
Growth & Income Allocation _____%

1.
2.
3.
Growth Allocation _____%

1.
2.
3.
Aggressive Growth Allocation _____%

1.
2.
3.
Safety Allocation (When You Are Nervous About Markets)

1.
2.